TACKLING TOUGH INTERVIEW QUESTIONS

BULLET GUIDE

Karen Mannering

Hodder Education, 338 Euston Road, London NW1 3BH

Hodder Education is an Hachette UK company

First published in UK 2011 by Hodder Education

This edition published 2011

Copyright © 2011 Karen Mannering

The moral rights of the author have been asserted

Database right Hodder Education (makers)

Artworks (internal and cover): Peter Lubach
Cover concept design: Two Associates

British Library Cataloguing in Publication Data: a catalogue record for this title is available from the British Library.

10 9 8 7 6 5 4 3 2 1

The publisher has used its best endeavours to ensure that any website addresses referred to in this book are correct and active at the time of going to press. However, the publisher and the author have no responsibility for the websites and can make no guarantee that a site will remain live or that the content will remain relevant, decent or appropriate.

The publisher has made every effort to mark as such all words which it believes to be trademarks. The publisher should also like to make it clear that the presence of a word in the book, whether marked or unmarked, in no way affects its legal status as a trademark.

Every reasonable effort has been made by the publisher to trace the copyright holders of material in this book. Any errors or omissions should be notified in writing to the publisher, who will endeavour to rectify the situation for any reprints and future editions.

Hachette UK's policy is to use papers that are natural, renewable and recyclable products and made from wood grown in sustainable forests. The logging and manufacturing processes are expected to conform to the environmental regulations of the country of origin.

www.hoddereducation.co.uk

Typeset by Stephen Rowling/Springworks

Printed in Spain

Contents

Acknowledgements

I would like to acknowledge all the personnel practitioners who have subjected me to some tough interview questions during my career. I would also like to thank Alison Frecknall and Victoria Roddam.

About the author

Karen Mannering lives in Kent and is a specialist in people development with over 20 years' experience. She has a degree in Psychology and a master's degree in Management Studies in addition to many skills-specific qualifications. She is a Fellow of the Institute of Personnel Development and a member of the British Psychological Society, the Chartered Management Institute and the Society of Women Writers and Journalists. Karen is also registered to use a wide range of psychometric tools to enhance her coaching.

Karen's enthusiasm for lifelong learning and people development, together with her background in management, results in a practical but humanistic approach to introducing training into the workplace. Karen has written many books on aspects of self-development. Her website can be found at www.karenmannering.co.uk.

Introduction

Imagine the scenario: you are excited to have been offered an interview for the job of your dreams. The interview has to be the easy bit – after all, they'll just want to **check a few things** and see if they like the look of you, right? Wrong!

Competition is fierce (there is only one job after all), and interview questions are tough. Any organization wants the best staff it can muster, and sets rigorous tests to identify exceptional candidates. However, it is not all down to chance. If you **prepare** and have some **strategies** in place, you can be more than ready for any tough or tricky question they ask you.

In this book I have gathered together a range of **tough questions**, complete with **fantastic answers**. When you start to understand the strategy behind the questions you'll also be able to create winning responses for yourself, tailored to your own personality and situation. This will give you more confidence and you will feel fully prepared for any eventuality and, of course, to **grab that job**!

1 Interview preparation

Before you get there

Interviews are **never easy**. Usually two or more people will be concentrating their attention completely on you and firing tough questions at you – questions that seem to be designed to catch you out.

It may seem that interviewers hold all the aces, but you have many cards you can play. The important thing is that, **before** you go to the interview, you've done all you can to be prepared.

Interviews are never easy

Interviews are a **necessary hurdle** to the job of your dreams, and as with all exercise, you'll benefit from training and preparation. This chapter explains how to:

* get in shape by doing your **homework**
* find out all you can about the **process**
* create the right **mindset** to meet the interviewer as an equal
* consider the **skills, knowledge** and **expertise** they'll be testing
* be ready with **fantastic responses** to those tough questions.

● Think of the interview as a hurdle…

The interview process

The *Concise Oxford Dictionary* defines 'interview' as:

i'**nterview**. Meeting of persons face to face, esp. for purpose of consultation; oral examination of candidate for employment, etc.

An interview is:	An interview is *not*:
a process for gaining views, thoughts and ideas	an opportunity to steamroller you
a way of testing knowledge and experience	the chance to highlight what you don't know
undertaken with positive intent: the interviewer wants to find the right candidate for the job	undertaken to make applicants look foolish

'Questions are never indiscreet. Answers sometimes are.'
Oscar Wilde

As part of the process you may be:

* interviewed by **one person** (usually the manager)
* interviewed by **a panel** – consisting of the manager, a personnel officer, any other interested party (such as a senior manager, shareholder or owner) and, in many cases in local government, members of the public.

Your interview could be:

* a **face-to-face interview**
* a **pre-interview by phone** followed by a face-to-face interview (often used when many applicants are anticipated or when the job requires telephone skills)
* a face-to-face interview accompanied by **tests** (questionnaires or ability tests)
* a full assessment at an **assessment centre**, where you undertake a number of tests over one or more days.

Create the right mindset

It is essential to begin creating the right mindset well before the interview happens, just in case you have telephone pre-screening before the actual interview, and to help you focus. Our behaviour starts with the way we think, and therefore to **behave and speak** confidently we have to **think and act** in a confident manner.

The outcome of acting and thinking with confidence	The implications of appearing to lack confidence
You can demonstrate an understanding of the job	You don't appear fully to understand the job
You appear keen and can start asking questions immediately and find out more	You may appear uninterested
You feel more prepared	You feel unprepared

The great thing about confidence is that you can 'fake it until you make it'. If you **act confident** you will feel confident – feel confident and it will come out in your actions, as shown by this virtuous circle.

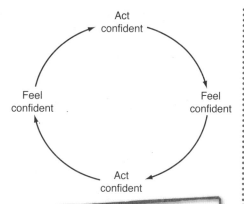

Act confident

Feel confident

Feel confident

Act confident

Remember

In an interview the power is not one-sided: interviews are a **two-way process**. You are essentially interviewing each other to see whether the fit feels right. Change your mindset to recognize that you are interviewing them too.

Do your homework

Don't leave your planning until the day of the interview – start **early**. You need to:

1 find out all you can about **the company** or business offering the job (look on the internet and ask for a company business plan)
2 research the **business sector** (e.g. service, oil industry, local government) and its likely future challenges (look on news sites and contact business magazines)
3 explore the **history** of the job. Is it a new role? Is someone leaving? Are they still there to ask? What are the likely challenges? (Could you contact people who already work there?)

The more homework you do, the more prepared you'll feel.

Remember
Recruiting people is hugely expensive for any organization so they want to get it right.

What are they testing?

As we have already established, interviews are a way of **testing information**. The recruiter will have your application form or CV, but needs to test out:

* your experience
* your background
* your reaction to some aspects of the job.

They will do this through the interview. In preparation you need to think through **what they might ask you**. Ask yourself:

1 Is there anything on your application form or CV that looks odd (a gap or a sudden change in career)?
2 Are there aspects of the job that you cannot evidence (e.g. this is for a management job but you have never managed people before)?
3 Do you appear over-qualified?

Think through your application

The interviewer will want to **clarify and test these issues** through questioning, so be brutal and compare the job description with your CV. Think through your application so you know where the mismatches are, and what skills, knowledge and abilities the interviewer will want to test.

The interviewer will also be looking to **confirm your experience**, so think of evidence you could provide (a project or outcome demonstrating your expertise).

● 'So how long were you involved in the mafia? Do you have any references?'

Case study

Casey has applied to be an entertainer in a theme park. She has a Performing Arts degree but no experience. She has not prepared, so when the telephone interview comes, she is caught unawares, forgets what she wrote in her application, and fails to give a telephone 'performance'. She is not shortlisted for the full interview.

Jason applies for the same job, but keeps a copy of his application by the phone, has thought through what he could bring to the role and how he can stand out from other entertainers. He asks a couple of sensible questions, and appears both interesting and interested. He is offered a face-to-face interview.

2 Answering the standard questions

Standard, but still challenging

There are some questions you should expect in any interview. However, **two mistakes** are commonly made:

* thinking that you don't need to prepare for such simple questions as 'Why do you want this job?' or 'What would you like to achieve while you are here?' After all, they're obvious, aren't they?
* thinking that you don't need to prepare for the interview at all.

Even standard questions require finely crafted answers
....

> **'You can tell whether a man is clever by his answers. You can tell whether a man is wise by his questions.'**
>
> Naguib Mahfouz

The questions on the previous page might appear to be standard, but even these apparently straightforward questions have more to them than meets the eye, and will require **finely crafted answers**. This chapter will help you to:

* **identify** some standard, or typical, questions
* **analyse** what is behind each question
* **prepare** some finely crafted answers
* **practise** your answers so that they flow naturally.

Identifying standard questions

These seemingly innocuous questions may appear at any time during an interview, but they are most likely to appear at the **beginning**, so that is where we should be ready for them.

At the beginning of an interview, it is considered best practice to ask some 'settling in' questions to aid the interviewee to start talking and to make them feel more comfortable – but these questions can still catch you out if you are not prepared.

Note!
This does not happen in high-pressure interviews or for internal and reorganization posts, where the candidates are known and time is of the essence.

Standard questions include:

* How was your journey here?
* Have you been here before?
* Talk me through the past five years of your work.
* Tell me how you came to be at this point in your life.

Don't assume that whoever shows you from the front door to the interview room is neutral. They could also be part of the process, so monitor your behaviour and the answers you give them as well.

● Watch out! The person who greets you at the door may not be all that they seem…

Analysing standard questions

Throughout this book we'll be attempting not only to answer questions effectively but also to identify the **key strategies** behind the questions. This approach will mean that, should the questioner veer away from the examples given here, you'll be able to identify the type of question they are using, and use the strategy to tailor your answer.

Although it's polite to settle an interviewee in and make them feel comfortable, these first questions have a further purpose: they give the interviewer **valuable information** from which they'll draw assumptions. It is for this reason that we must not take the questions at face value, and we must dig a little deeper.

Don't take the questions at face value

The standard questions are of two main types:

Type 1

'How was your journey here?' and 'Have you been here before?' sound chatty, but:

* the first is testing how you'd be at turning up every day (especially relevant if you live far away)
* the second is testing whether you've applied to the company before – and also (if they already know this) how honest you are.

Type 2

'Talk me though the past five years of your work' and 'Tell me how you came to be at this point in your life' again sound chatty, but the interviewer wants to find out how you feel you can make the leap from your current job to this one.

Answering standard questions

Some neat answers for the standard questions given would be:

Type 1

'How was your journey here?'

* 'My journey was fine, thank you.' (Keep your answer **positive** and stay away from anything negative such as 'It took much longer than I thought.')

'Have you been here before?'

* Answer **honestly**. If you have attended another interview at the same place, say so, but don't state any opinion on either the job you were applying for or anyone involved in the process.

● 'My journey? Absolutely terrible – I wouldn't like to do that every day!'

Type 2

'Talk me through the past five years of your work.'

* 'Well, five years ago I was working for a chemical company as a team leader, but I knew I needed to move if I were to progress, so I...' – only the past five years are relevant to your current skills, and they are looking for **links** and **progression**.

'Tell me how you came to be at this point in your life.'

* This is for someone changing career. Emphasize your career history and give a **strong, positive** reason for changing ('I saw an opportunity in this sector...').

'Would you like a drink?'

* Don't read anything into this; they are probably just being polite, so if you want one, have one.

Practise, practise

Your answers need to flow – and the only way to do this is to practise.

Practising regularly will:

✔ enable your responses to flow
✔ ensure that even you believe your responses 100 per cent
✔ give you confidence to be able to tailor your answers to other similar questions
✔ enable you to make sure your answers relate to the job you are applying for.

Don't bother to practise and you will:

✘ stumble over your answers
✘ feel awkward, especially if you know you are glossing over something
✘ fall apart if the interviewer does not ask exactly the 'right' questions.

22

Case study

Lena has an interview at an insurance company. She has difficulty finding the building, and the receptionist is dismissive towards her. When asked, 'Did you find the offices all right?' she answers, 'I found the map confusing and your receptionist a bit rude.' Although aware of the issues, the interviewer finds her comments abrasive and tactless.

Leno goes for the same interview and also has problems finding the venue, but when asked the same question, he answers, 'Yes, fine thank you.' He reasons that, now he knows where the offices are, he'll find them again quickly, and will mention the receptionist's behaviour if he gets the job. To the interviewer he comes across as affable and pleasant.

3 Questions about qualifications and experience

Asking about qualifications and experience

The CV or application form you submitted for the job focuses primarily on your career history and qualifications. It does not always detail the level of your experience.

You may have worked in a team, but what size was it? What did you actually *do*? This is why an interviewer will be testing your **level of experience**, to see whether you really are capable of doing this new job.

An interviewer will be testing your level of experience

This chapter looks at some **real examples** of tough questions relating to your qualifications and experience. For your own situation, you will need to:

* read each question and **adapt** it for your own industry or position
* think about what the interview is **trying to find out** (an example is given with each question)
* think of the **evidence** for all that you say.

If your answer is interesting, the interviewer may say, 'That's interesting, why do you say that?' In this case you will need to plan what you would answer.

Qualifications and experience – what's the difference?

The simple answer is that a qualification often gives you a bit of paper, while experience does not. However, the reality goes deeper than this. Qualifications and experience go hand in hand, and therefore interviewers are looking for **BOTH**.

* **Your qualifications** demonstrate that you have knowledge of the theory necessary to undertake certain tasks.
* **Your experience** demonstrates that you have actually done these things with real people, over time.

● To climb the job ladder you need both knowledge and experience…

If you lie at interview, you will be found out and your credibility will be
in tatters. If you don't have the qualifications you need, major on your
experience – but only if it is **real and justifiable** (the company may well
ring up your current employer to check out the details).

If you have neither qualifications nor experience for the job of your
dreams, set your sights slightly lower for now and resolve to gain both as
soon as you can.

'Experience enables you to recognize a mistake when you make it again.'

Franklin P. Jones

The strategy – what's being asked here, and why?

The interviewer wants to test out:

1 whether you have actually done a job like this before
2 whether you are a 'safe pair of hands' or whether you need nurturing
3 your level or depth of experience
4 whether you are willing and prepared to take this next step.

You should be aiming to put the interviewer's mind at rest by persuading them that **they can have confidence in you** (through your examples). It is crucial to sell yourself at this point because you may have a spread of experience from a number of different jobs.

Top tip
Give examples of your specific achievements, successes and problems overcome.

Case study

Kim has gone for a job in fashion retail. She hasn't thought about the interview, expecting that they'll want her to talk about fashion. When the interviewer asks, 'Why should I give you the job when there are six other applicants outside who also love fashion?' Kim crumbles. Forgetting all her experience and qualifications, she stammers, 'I don't know…' and is not offered a second interview.

Mark was among those sitting outside. Asked the same question, he answers, 'I've experience in retail, and my qualifications include customer care and maths. I have a customer-friendly attitude and I can use electronic tills and stock ordering software.' Mark is offered a second interview.

Tough questions about qualifications

Here are some **tough questions** and **possible answers**:

'Why do you have such a wide range of qualifications?'

- ✳ You are being asked to justify your career path. 'I have always been a keen learner and believe in spreading my learning over a wider area than, perhaps, other people. This has enabled me to draw concepts from a wider field.'

'How have these qualifications helped in your work so far?'

- ✳ This is a particularly testing question. 'I applied a theory we covered in my diploma to help with a team change in my last position. I find many theories quite helpful in my work.'

'How good is your maths/English?'

* Regrettably, having a qualification does not necessarily confirm a high level of literacy or numeracy. You may have a degree in marketing, yet still be poor at mathematics. **Be honest** and explain what was included in the course, with examples.

'Do you feel there is anything missing in your qualification list?'

* If something is obviously missing then say so, and mention that you would like to **work towards it**. Otherwise, say, 'I have found that my qualifications have provided a sufficiently wide level of knowledge for me so far in my career.'

'If you were to choose one qualification that you believe critical for this job, which would it be?'

* Make sure it's one you have: 'I think it would be… because it prepared me for many different situations.'

Tough questions about experience

Here are some further tough questions and possible answers, this time about your experience:

'What makes you think you have the right experience for this job?'

* This is slightly **challenging**, but not too difficult. 'I think I have the right level of experience because in my previous role I managed the team while my manager was away, and dealt with a whole host of staffing issues.'

'What mistakes have you made in your previous job?'

* Do not say 'None' – it is never true. The trick is to state a mistake but make it a fairly minor one, and one from which you have **learned**.

34

'What has been your greatest achievement?'

* Don't say anything personal such as 'Having my children', even if it's true. Again, be ready for this one and have an example up your sleeve. You could say something like 'Developing other people and seeing them grow', but just make sure you can back this up with **an example**!

'Rate yourself on a scale of 1 to 10.'

* This is a **direct challenge**. Don't go too high (and seem arrogant) or too low (otherwise why are you there?). 'I would say around an 8 and working towards a 9 – I am a constant work in progress.'

'What have you done that showed initiative (or drove the company forward)?'

* They are looking for your 'X factor' here. This is a common question in a fast-paced industry, so have an example ready – something that saved money or increased sales.

4 Questions about gaps in your CV and career changes

CV gaps and career changes

Your CV may not fully flow in date sequence. Interviewers will look for gaps in career history, so have **explanations** ready. Some interviewers are suspicious of anything other than consistent full-time employment.

The same is true for **sudden career changes**. To you, these changes were a way of testing different careers, but to an interviewer they may indicate that you don't know what you want and might leave them after a short time.

Interviewers will look for CV gaps and career changes

Taking on a new employee is a **huge investment**, and an interviewer will not take a risk on someone if they are at all unsure, or feel that they might leave the company after a few months. To alleviate that fear, you will need to:

* recognize where there may be **issues** or concerns that the interviewer will raise
* prepare a **positively phrased statement** to use early on in the interview
* create **positive links** from your other jobs to the one you are seeking
* ensure that you have **solid reasons** for your actions
* show enthusiasm for the job for which you are applying.

Explaining gaps in your CV

There are many reasons for having gaps in your CV. Some will appear **positive**, while others will be perceived as **negative**. For example, you could have taken time out for the following reasons:

Perceived as positive reasons	Perceived as negative reasons
A sabbatical or form of study	In prison
Raising a family or caring for others	Very poor health
Travelling	Appearing work-shy or difficult to place

If you have had a break in your career history, it is important to highlight this on your CV, but **how you present this** is crucial.

'Nobody can go back and start a new beginning, but anyone can start today and make a new ending.'
Maria Robinson

Top tip

Don't be tempted to lie. Joining up dates will only work if you are talking about a few days, not months, and if you are found out you will lose your job.

If possible, enter on your CV the reason for the gap. For example:

'July 2006 – June 2007 – Career break to look after an elderly relative' 41

This way everything is **upfront** and already displayed to the interviewer.

If this is not possible (or you don't wish to disclose the reason), raise it in the interview – 'As you can see I was unemployed between [date] and [date]. This was due to…' – and then present the reason as positively (but still truthfully) as possible.

Questions about gaps in your CV

Apart from 'There are gaps in your CV, can you explain them?' other questions might be:

'How much absence have you had in the past five years?'

* This is a way of finding out whether you have taken much time out for **illness**. The interviewer will contact your former employer, so be honest and explain the situation.

'It appears you had a career break at this time; how did you stay up to date?'

* The interviewer is questioning your **current knowledge**. Mention journals read, relevant programmes watched, courses undertaken or other learning: 'Yes I was away for two years but during that time I undertook some distance learning programmes such as…'

'What challenges did you face when you came back into employment?'

* The interviewer wants to see whether you'll **fit in easily** with other team members. Say something positive like, 'I had to integrate myself back into team work after being on my own for so long.'

'Why do you think you've been out of work for so long?'

* This is a direct challenge – **do not buckle!** 'I believe that employment is such a large part of life that it has to be right. A position like this has simply not come up before now.'

● The questions may be challenging…but keep calm!

Explaining a career change

There are **many reasons** why we might change career:

* The career we had has simply disappeared. (Is anyone left in the typing pool?)
* The career was not what we thought from the outside. (Modelling is not all glamour.)
* The work is sporadic. (You might be a session singer.)
* We found we did not fit in. (You might have been in sales when you aren't an extrovert.)
* We become bored and want to try something new.

As with gaps in your CV, don't try to hide this. You'll need to think through the **positive aspects** of your career changes and **find the thread** that runs through your employment history.

Case study

Phil left school with few qualifications but could not get a job. He tried for jobs, but was not called for interview. Time seemed to slip by. However, Phil now decides to view this period as a time when he was researching companies before applying to his first employer and getting a job – and suddenly that seems more positive.

Tessa left the civil service to become a therapist, and now is trying for a job in telephone customer services. Rather than view her career as fragmented, Tessa tells the interviewer that it has followed a steady path of customer service. Her interviewer sees the connection and asks for more information.

Questions about a career change

Since the company is interested enough in you to have offered you an interview, you can make a feature of your previous experience. If the opportunity arises, tackle it head on by saying, 'As you can see, I've had **a variety of experience**, and I believe this has contributed towards my development so far.'

In other words, change it into a positive element that other candidates won't have. Now look at whether there is **a tangible theme** throughout all your previous roles, such as customer care, implementing a quality service or IT – and promote that. In essence, you are creating **a dedicated career thread** where there was possibly happenstance.

Make a feature of your previous experience

Here are some tricky questions you might have to face if you've had a varied career path:

'What have you learned through having these different jobs?'

* This is **a helpful question** – the interviewer is asking you to make that positive thread. You should state the connection: 'As you can see, all my work has been in customer care.'

'Why have you changed career so many times?'

* This is a challenge again. You need to give a good reason if you are not to be labelled fickle. 'I'll be bringing a hugely diverse range of learning into this role, which will make me a much better manager.'

● Don't just say you got bored – give positive reasons for changing career.

5 Questions using a competency framework

What's a competency framework?

Competency frameworks are not about qualifications but about the **behaviour and skills** expected from staff.

Many organizations use competency frameworks, and if the organization interviewing you has one you will be marked in line with it at your interview. Competency frameworks can give you **clues** about the questions they'll ask and where they'll be placing their attention.

> **'Competence goes beyond words. It's the leader's ability to say it, plan it, and do it in such a way that others know that you know how – and know that they want to follow you.'**
>
> John C. Maxwell

Competency frameworks are about assessing behaviour and skills

Before every interview, it will pay you to:

* find out whether the company has a competency framework
* where it might overlap with **your own professional standards**
* consider how those competencies may be tested through questions
* feed **competency-specific replies** back to the interviewer.

Why have a competency framework?

Staff recruitment was once based on whether candidates could do tasks such as type and use a computer. Today most people can do this, and organizations need **other measures** if they are to select the best candidates.

As a way of helping them stand out, many companies also decided to add to their brand by saying, 'We want to employ this type of person or someone who shows these specific skills.'

● In today's competitive working environment you have to be able to demonstrate multiple skills…

52

Most competencies are based around what we call **soft skills** such as how we communicate – not factual (or hard) skills like whether you can write a report or not.

Competency frameworks are now in place in most large organizations and local government. They allow the employer to:

* recruit the **right type** of person for the company
* tailor their **in-house training** to meet any competency deficits
* create a **management programme** that fits the organization
* pay (or reward) staff for **development** of certain competencies
* create a unique **company culture**.

Competency frameworks help measure the qualities that a company feels it needs to fit its approach, for example, having a customer focus. They also help employees to be clear about how they are expected to perform in their jobs.

Competency frameworks and professional standards

If you are in a profession with a code of conduct or professional standards, you will be expected to work to **both** sets of standards. This may come up during an interview question such as:

'I notice that you are a professional manager. How do the standards of your institute agree or conflict with our competency framework?'

* If you are unprepared, this will leave you open-mouthed. Make sure you compare professional standards/competencies with any company-specific ones *before* the interview.
* If you have not done this, your best answer would be, 'The essence of all standards is working to **best practice principles** and in that they are very similar.'

Competencies usually have **headings** followed by **supporting elements** that go into more detail.

Customer care means different things in different industries, but as an example, let's take the competency framework of a small office:

A customer focus:

1 ensures all customers (internal and external) are dealt with in a pleasant manner
2 replies to all letters within 48 hours
3 returns all phone calls on the day of the call
4 creates a problem-solving approach with the customer.

Can you transfer these statements into possible questions?

Look on the following page.

Extracting questions from competencies

If you were to apply for a job in the small office cited on the previous page, and customer care was an essential element of that job, the interviewer will be **testing you against these elements**, asking you to prove by your actions that you have the competency. Therefore the questioning could go:

'Tell me what customer care means to you.'

✳ testing 1, 2, 3 and 4

'How long do you think it's acceptable to leave a customer once they have rung in or written to us?'

✳ testing 2 and 3

'If a customer rings in and says a product is late, what would you say to them?'

✳ testing 4.

You can see that competency-based questions require you to show how you either would or did **deal with a situation**:

'Give an example of where you have increased productivity in your last role.'

This question is testing you to see whether you were:

✳ truly engaged within your last company and cared about output
✳ just an attendee – doing the job but without commitment.

Your response can be fairly brief: 'I noticed [demonstrating **engagement**] that the samples were collected on a day when we're trying to get the notices out. This caused confusion, so I suggested moving one of them to another day [**personal action**], and the result was fewer mistakes made [**the outcome**].'

More competency-based questions

These general questions aim to find out more about your interpersonal and communication skills.

'Give me an example of when you dealt with conflict in your team.'

* The interviewer wants to know how you react to **team conflict,** so don't say that you have never come up against conflict; instead, say, 'Conflict can occur because people feel passionately about their work – they both want to please the customer. I try to get them to see that actually they're on the same side.'

'What is your favoured method of communication?'

* Most competency frameworks address **communication** problems. Answer, 'My preferred method is always face to face but I understand that this is not always possible if people are in a different office or country.'

Case study

Peter has asked company X about its standards and any competency framework. They have sent him details and he has found more on their website. Peter looks at the behaviour and skills the company wants and prepares possible questions from the competencies. He knows they may still catch him out, but feels confident that he fits their 'mould' of employee.

Sinéad decides she doesn't have time to contact the company or look on its website – after all, she reasons, if she's right for it, she'll get the job. She soon realizes, during the interview, that the panel want her to show specific qualities, and she wishes she'd known that in advance.

6 Questioning your attitude

Attitude and personality

Like it or not, you bring your **personality** to work. If you have a poor attitude towards the company or your work, you'll struggle to find your place and it will cause problems with other staff.

Everyone is different – some people like a dynamic environment and others a quiet life – and an interviewer will try to ascertain whether you have the **right attitude** for the role on offer.

Like it or not, you bring your personality to work

●●

Whatever job you do, you have to work with other people, and your attitude is important in ensuring that you fit into the **ethos** of the workplace. The right attitude cannot be bought, and so personal insight is essential. We need to:

* know how our attitude **affects others**
* understand how **changing** our attitude is in our hands
* be prepared to **rethink** our attitude if necessary
* be aware of how attitude is **screened** during the interview process.

This chapter looks at attitude and where it comes from, and the questions you might be asked about attitude at interview.

What is attitude?

Our personality is made up from the many facets of ourselves, and our attitude is part of that mix. However, our attitude can change.

64

Imagine your partner said to meet you in a dingy old pub for a meal. You might enter the pub thinking that you don't want to spend an evening in there, let alone eat. Your face is sour and you feel disappointed. You know you won't enjoy the evening.

Then your partner comes in and says, 'Get your coat, we are eating in the French restaurant next door.' Suddenly your attitude towards the evening changes, and you feel upbeat. It's going to be a great night.

Why attitude is important

In that example, our attitude altered in response to the surroundings; but what if you have a very **negative attitude** towards customers, clients, or even work in general? That might result in you giving out all the wrong signals and driving customers away from you.

It might also make the workplace **difficult for other people**.

'Attitude is a little thing that makes a big difference.'
Winston Churchill

● In the workplace a person with a bad attitude can cause problems…

Where your attitude comes from

Your attitude comes from **experiences** you have had in life, right back to childhood. If you have a negative attitude towards anything, for example people in senior positions, it's worth trying to think back to any negative experience you may have had that would have fuelled this.

> **Top tip**
> **Only you** can change your attitude to anything or anyone – no one else can do it for you, so do some reflection if you think this is an area where you may not fare well.

Attitudes are **contagious**. Staff members with a good attitude have moved mountains, while it only takes one person with a poor attitude to bring down an entire team.

Employers are more likely to employ staff with a positive attitude towards their work. People with the right attitude fit into the team and become **productive workers**. Essentially:

Staff with a good attitude:	Staff with a poor attitude:
lift the morale of others	lower morale for everyone
solve problems with their 'can do' approach	leave problems unsolved
get a great deal from their work	value only monetary reward from work

● …but a good attitude will lift your team's morale

'Tell me about yourself...'

This is the **classic attitude question** and is often fearful to candidates. What do you say? What are they looking for? If you are asked this question:

✔ *Be brief*
✔ *Give a snapshot of your career to date*
✔ *Only include outside information such as hobbies, sport or volunteering*
✘ *Don't chat on for ages*
✘ *Don't talk about personal situations*
✘ *Don't talk about relationships, family or pets*

Better still, **be prepared**. Have a **30-second summary** that you have already practised and honed. This is such a popular question that you are bound to come across it at some point in your career.

68

Here are some variations on the theme:

'How would you describe yourself?'

* This neat question is looking for some level of **self-appraisal**. This is your sales pitch, but be careful not to appear arrogant. 'I believe I am a highly trained extrovert who works hard to achieve the best for my organization.'

'How would others describe you?'

* For this twist on the question above use the voice of your manager: 'My current role incorporates a fair amount of personal feedback and my manager said recently that he found me a very able and popular member of the team.'

'How do you feel about routine tasks?'

* Every job has a certain number of **routine tasks,** and your attitude towards them is crucial: 'I think that routine tasks have their place in every organization and I find that they often make a pleasant diversion from the more demanding tasks.'

Playful 'attitude' questions

The interviewer will be judging your motivation and attitude through these seemingly playful questions.

'If you were an animal, what would you be?'

* Try not to give a playful answer! Think of an animal that represents the qualities you wish to promote: 'I think I'd be a bear because they are big and dependable.'

'If you had all the money in the world, and all the ability and qualifications, what would you be?'

* This question seeks to understand what your **ultimate job** would be and how far away from it you are. Try something like: 'I'd probably be in the same industry [**staying power**] but owning my own organization [**ambition**]. I'd be free to promote the product and possibly start a charity arm of the business [**socially responsible**].'

Case study

Lionel hasn't bothered to think about attitude. It's only an interview for an administration post so he feels his attitude doesn't really matter. Consequently when the interviewer starts asking Lionel attitudinal questions, he gives flippant answers. He's not called back for a second interview.

Amy desperately wants the administration post. She is keen and efficient but shy. However, she has thought through some questions and when the interviewer says, 'Tell me about yourself,' Amy has rehearsed a neat and witty reply. She's aware that the interview is not just about what she does but also the person she is at work. Amy is asked back for a second interview.

7 Questioning your potential

Why question potential?

An interview is not just about what you know and can do now. Your interviewers will be looking for **potential**, and to see whether you would be **a good investment** for their company.

It costs a great deal to employ a member of staff and familiarize them with the company sufficiently for them to become an effective and efficient worker, possibly with a long-term career with their organization.

Interviewers will be looking for potential, and to see whether you would be a good investment

Looking at your potential may mean that the organization is thinking about grooming you for promotion, or it may be aiming for you to achieve complete mastery at your current level.

To ensure that your potential is always uppermost in your mind during an interview, you will need to:

* recognize a question that incorporates **an indication of potential**
* match this to where the company indicates its **growth areas**
* demonstrate responses that are in line with the **company's vision**
* indicate **specific areas** where you feel your career is progressing.

'Focus on your potential instead of your limitations.'
Alan Loy McGinnis

The way we work now

The days of working for **one organization** our whole life are behind us. Whether you see this as a problem or not, it does have some advantages. Workers today are **free** to move to any organization or company they want, and need not feel trapped somewhere where they are unhappy or fearful of poor references if they move.

This greater movement of staff has resulted in companies having to change their expectations. They no longer see staff as being there for 30 years, and so are looking only for potential growth over **five to ten years**. In other words, they see their (and your) investment over a much shorter timescale.

Potential is not always for promotion or management – you can have the potential to be a great worker at any level

Assessing your potential

Potential is not always for promotion or management – you can have the potential to be a great worker at any level. To assess potential, interviewers will therefore be asking themselves:

* How **fast** can we get you up and running (time = money)?
* How **efficient** will you be (how soon will our investment be repaid)?
* How **much** will you need spent on you (training and/or qualifications)?
* How can we keep you as **long** as is practical (what inducements will make you stay)?

● In part, an organization will want to hire you for your potential...

Questions about personal potential

Whether you move up the corporate ladder or not, you always have the potential to expand on your own personal skills. Demonstrating personal potential shows a **willingness to learn** and incorporate those skills back into your work.

Example questions may be:

'What are your weaknesses, and what do you expect to do about them?'

* You need self-analysis here, and an indication that you intend to close any gaps. What you disclose should be easy to remedy, so never say anything too damning: 'One of my weaknesses is that I am a perfectionist. I need to learn that, in some instances, good enough is good enough.'

'You weren't promoted by your previous organization. Why is that?'

✳ The interviewer may suspect that you are **not as good as your CV says**, and wants to test this out. 'My previous employer was a family-run organization. They did not promote anyone outside the family. Now I want to work for a professional organization that promotes those who deliver results.'

'Where do you see yourself in five years' time?'

✳ This question is open to interpretation. Keep the response simple: 'I will still be employed [**commitment**], working in a job I enjoy [**integrity**], but hopefully with more skills and more responsibility [**personal growth**].'

> Personal potential indicates **personal growth**.

Questions about practical potential

This is assessing potential focused on your **practical ability**. The classic question is:

'If you were offered a job here, where do you see your career going, both short and long term?'

Do say:

- ✔ I see myself as learning and settling in my role for the first year.
- ✔ I want to take all the opportunities presented, and find out more about the company.
- ✔ Long term, I see myself in a more senior role in a company like this, but only when I'm ready.

Don't say:

- ✘ I see myself on a fast track to the next job.
- ✘ Long term, I want to be in a senior position, running a department or on the Board.
- ✘ I want your job.

Other questions of this type might be:

'Given your background, aren't you being unrealistic about your career aspirations?'

  ✳ This challenging comment is dressed up as being practical. The interviewer wants to check your reaction, so **keep calm**: 'No, I don't believe I am. Human potential is vast and I believe anyone can achieve their aims.'

'I see that you have qualifications and have attended courses. Which has been the most beneficial to you so far?'

  ✳ The interviewer is trying to see where your **interest** lies. 'I've found all my training and development fascinating, but I think the most beneficial has been working on the job with other people. That's where I've learned most.'

Career progression and ambition

Assess the company you are applying to and the role before you mention being ambitious; it is not always viewed as a good quality.

'How important is career progression to you?'

* They could be testing you to find out your **intentions** or because there is no career progression from this position. 'It depends what you mean by career progression. If you mean learning and developing, it's very important, but if you mean climbing the corporate ladder, I think it's a little early to discuss that.'

In a large company, ambition is fine. There are so many departments you can move into to keep you interested and pursuing a more senior role.

In a small company (or when applying for a head of department role) there is often **no further progression**. In this situation, mention that you are ambitious and it might go against you. The interviewer will assume you'll soon be bored (since the company cannot offer you further progression opportunities) and leave – affecting their investment in you.

Case study

Rose is ambitious; she wants to make management by the time she is 30, and sees moving from job to job as the way to achieve this. The interviewer is suspicious: why doesn't she stay in any one position? Perhaps she's been promoted beyond her ability and is moving from job to job before she is caught out. Rose never realized that this was the message her CV was giving.

Simon is extremely laid back. He never sees any reason to push for any type of advancement, even though he has management qualifications. The interviewer is suspicious again because he should be applying for a supervisory role, rather than administration.

8 Being interviewed for a promotion

What to expect

Not all interviews are about new people entering a business or trying for a job at entry level. An interview can be for a promotion within the same company or any other type of **internal selection**.

All organizations need to put in place **a fair and equitable process** for deciding who is awarded a promotion or given an opportunity to work on an esteemed project.

Interviews for a promotion need to be challenging because they must stand up to scrutiny

> **'You see things; and you say, "Why?" But I dream things that never were; and I say, "Why not?"'**
>
> George Bernard Shaw

Interviews for a promotion need to be **vigorous and challenging** because they must stand up to scrutiny. By introducing a fair system, the company will be able to demonstrate that they chose the candidate on merit, not favouritism. Therefore we need to:

* expect the questions to be more **probing**
* recognize that **higher-level** jobs need more experience, knowledge and leadership
* be willing to **stretch ourselves** and move out of our comfort zone
* sell ourselves with solid confidence.

Sell yourself with confidence

There's no point in attempting a promotion interview if you are not willing to sell yourself and **promote your abilities** with confidence. Part of pushing ahead in your career is being able to push your talents forward too.

The truth is that if you don't do this, another candidate will, and they will get the job. Even if the person interviewing you knows you, you must still **state your case**, and convince the interviewer that they should choose you.

● To gain a promotion, you need to promote yourself…

Show them what drives you

Not everyone pushes for promotion in the hope of more money. Some people:

* want to **change** the way their company is run
* need to feel a **champion** of the people
* believe **passionately** in a product and how it is developed
* feel they have natural **leadership qualities** that excite people to follow them.

However, if they don't articulate this in the interview, their moment will be lost. To be fair, the outcome must be based on what happens in the interview itself, and not on a conversation that happened a few weeks earlier.

Even if the person interviewing you knows you, you must still state your case

Prepare for the task

Many people seriously underestimate the size of the step up involved in being promoted. It is not just about earning more money; you need **ability** and **charisma**, to be a **risk taker** and also **a safe pair of hands**. It is a constant juggling act and, if you are at all concerned, it's a good idea to ask to shadow another manager for a day.

In preparation, make sure you know your company **business plan** inside out, and understand the financial planning details. For example, you may be asked about the impact of moving business to another country, so you need to have thought about such details.

> **Top tip**
> Look and sound as though you are ready for bigger things and you will find that bigger things come to you.

The task of **management** can be challenging, and you'll need all that confidence mentioned previously, to carry you through. There is also the issue that increasingly companies are producing flatter structures by stripping out layers of management.

That means that there will be **fewer managers** managing **bigger teams**. It is not for the faint hearted – and that is why the interview will be:

* testing
* rigorous
* challenging.

● Make sure you know the business and financial plans inside out…

The likely questions

Rigorous questions

'How will you establish immediate authority?'

* They are looking for **strength** and **leadership**. 'I know the team will have been without a leader for some time and therefore I'd introduce myself and have one-to-one meetings with everyone to establish their roles. I'd then...'

'How would you describe your management style?'

* If you have done a psychometric you may have an answer already but if not, 'I believe I'm firm but fair. The company has to come first, but I want my staff to like working here so that we all benefit from the enjoyment of work.'

'How much do you want this job?'

* Be careful – they are looking for keenness, but in a measured way.

Testing questions

'What's wrong in this company?'

* Don't be too honest in your reply! Try, 'I think all companies have areas where they could be improved – for example in communication. That is a small area with large ramifications when it goes wrong...'

'If money were no object, where would you take the company next?'

* Think carefully here and be sensible; don't go for world domination: 'Perhaps I would experiment with a new product in a different country. I feel that we have the capacity to take on brave new areas of business.'

'What's your opinion of the company's growth predictions for next year?'

* Again, honesty is not always best: 'I think they are ambitious, especially considering the current financial climate, but certainly something strong to work towards. They give tremendous focus.'

Challenging questions

'What stresses you out?'/'What makes you angry?'

* They are looking for how far you can be **pushed**. Don't say 'Nothing' – that's never true. Try, 'Ingratitude (or lack of consideration) in others. I work hard to enable other people to enjoy their work but find it difficult to understand when they don't care.'

'What sacrifices are you willing to make to succeed?'

* They are asking you **how far you'd go**. Don't tell them you'd do anything. Try, 'I'm willing to make big sacrifices with my time. For this role to be a success I accept that I'll need to work unsocial hours from time to time, and I'm prepared for that.'

94

Case study

Chris wants a promotion because his manager seems always to be in his room drinking tea. It's got to be an easy job! Chris has some qualifications but does little research before the interview. He cannot understand why he is not called back for further discussions.

Christine works in the same team but asks to shadow another manager for the day to get an idea of her work. Christine sees the breadth of the role and asks many questions. The manager gives Christine a business plan to read and explains the financial side in detail. Christine is delighted to be offered a chance for further discussions.

9 Questions work both ways

Asking your own questions

During your interview you will want to find out more about the position on offer. Asking for **clarification** as you go along is fine, but leave in-depth questions **until the end**, as the interviewer might cover these topics anyway.

There is no problem with making **a few notes** during an interview, but don't write down anything other than key points, and keep your focus on the interview itself.

Preparation is the key to asking well-crafted questions

'Sometimes questions are more important than answers.'

Nancy Willard

Preparation is the key to asking well-crafted questions. It's fine to have made a few notes beforehand and use them in the interview, as it's easy for your mind to go blank when you are nervous.

You'll need to think about:

* what you **want to know** (if there are gaps in the data they have provided)
* what your questions say about **you** (is it detail or strategic?)

Jot down a few questions on **cue cards** to take in with you.

Putting the interview in perspective

Although this book concentrates on the tough questions you may be asked, remember that the interview works **both ways**.

It's not unusual, during an interview, to come to the conclusion that you would not accept the job if it were offered to you. This is because the interview is a two-way process: it is essentially a **fact-finding mission** between two people to see whether each thinks the other fits their future agenda.

If you are **nervous**, thinking about it in this way can help. You are interviewing the company as much as they are interviewing you, and remembering this can help you keep **a level head**.

● 'I've decided against it...'

Questions before the interview

Whenever I am advising anyone in respect of a job interview I always recommend that they:

1 find out as much about the company and job before the interview
2 seek out the manager for a chat prior to the interview.

The first is to find out as much detail as possible so that you can place your answers in context and formulate **intelligent questions**. The second is so that you can find out the **vision** held by the manager (and try to impress by being proactive).

Warning
Not all managers will meet candidates before the interview. Some feel it would give some candidates an unfair advantage over others.

Questions at the end of the interview

At the end of any interview the interviewer will usually ask whether you have any questions you would like to ask. This has **two aspects**:

1 whether you still have **any outstanding questions** about the job and what will be expected of you – the interview cannot cover everything and there may be areas where you need clarification about certain details
2 whether you ask **an intelligent question** – the question you ask will reveal more about you than you think (remember, the interview is not over yet).

Warning
'When do I start?' implies that you think you already have the job.
'What other perks are there in this job?' implies that you are only interested in the benefits, not the work itself.

Types of question to ask

Questions may seem such easy, short and simple things but there is more to them than you might initially suspect. Asking intelligent questions will show that you are committed and taking the job and the organization seriously.

There are several **categories** of question that you could ask the interviewer, but let's concentrate on **three** particular types and see them in action:

1 open questions
2 closed questions
3 probing questions.

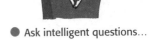

● Ask intelligent questions…

Open questions

Use open questions to encourage an **expansive** reply.

Example open questions	Example replies
I have read the business plan, but can you tell me how the business initially came into being?	Yes, the company was started in 1970 by our current chairman, Paul Hendry. It was initially based in Salford but moved to...
Can you explain how the appraisal system works?	Every March each manager undertakes an appraisal with every team member...
I understand that the company holds a conference once a year. Can you explain that to me?	Every year the company hosts the annual Chartered Engineering Conference. This event is something that we expect everyone to...

Closed questions

Use closed questions when you want **short, sharp** replies or detail. They need not be hard; they are mainly reserve questions for extracting **facts**.

Example closed questions	Example replies
How many people are currently in the team?	Five.
Do you anticipate that the company will be moving into exports in the coming year?	No, not next year.
Who is responsible for your quality checks?	Mr Gifford.

● It's fine to make a few notes beforehand…

Probing questions

Use probing questions when you want to **know more** about (or wish to dig deeper into) something.

Example probing questions	Example replies
You mentioned that the company supports a local charity. Can you tell me more about that?	Smilies Trust? Yes, of course. It was founded in [date] in response to…
In your business plan there's a section on international business; can you tell me a bit more about what this involves?	Of course; the international office is based in [city] and every employee has the opportunity to visit there at least once…
Did you just mention a share offer? Can you tell me about that?	Every employee is given…

Case study

Jamil has made a list of questions he would like to ask at the end of the interview. He recognizes that what he asks says a lot about him as an employee, and so he deletes some of the more obvious questions, and refines the others.

Carol knows what questions she wants to ask but has not made a note of them, and during the interview forgets what they were. She knows she must ask something, so blurts out, 'When will I hear whether I have been successful?' Although this question is not terrible, she could kick herself because she had some good questions in her mind yesterday.

10 Assessment centres

The purpose of assessment centres

If you are applying for a senior appointment, expect your interview to be at an assessment centre. Assessment centres attempt to capture data on candidates from a full **360-degree perspective**, with questioning a part of that.

If you are asked to attend an assessment centre you need to be aware of the skills observers will look for, and how to **impress them** by performing, answering questions and monitoring your behaviour.

Assessment centres capture data on candidates from a 360-degree perspective

The key to performing well in assessment centres is to:

* research the company and the core competencies they are looking for, as for any other interview
* think in depth **beforehand** – what could they ask you to do and what aspects of the job are they likely to test?
* formalize some easy responses to any questions about **the process** (e.g. 'Did you enjoy that activity?')
* **engage fully** in the activities (they will mark you down if you are silent)
* ultimately, **be yourself** – if they want to employ you they'll want the real you, not someone good at performing in assessment centres.

What happens at an assessment centre?

Assessment centres are usually aimed at **senior appointments** because, although the centres are expensive to run, the cost of getting it wrong is higher. This makes them a good investment.

Assessment centres may run over **one or two days**, and often involve a fair amount of sitting around. You'll be observed all the time – not just when you are performing – and your questions noted.

Due to the high cost of employing the wrong candidate, assessment centres are a worthwhile investment

● At an assessment centre you will be under close scrutiny…

What do you do in an assessment centre?

An assessment centre is made up of a number of **activities** – whatever is pertinent to the job. These activities might include:

* psychometric tests – for personality profiling
* numerical and literacy tests – to test budgeting and literacy
* practical tests – such as writing a report
* a team activity – such as planning something in a group
* a debating activity – such as candidates bidding for money against each other
* a media interview or recording – often for those taking up public office
* a presentation – to test your presentation skills
* role-play exercises – to test communication skills
* in-tray exercises – to test your ability to prioritize, organize, plan and schedule work

...and of course **an interview**.

What are they looking for?

Assessment centres are usually quite tough. The organizers will expect you to move from activity to activity seamlessly, and therefore they are also testing your **flexibility** and how you cope **under pressure**.

A typical assessment centre will have a grid of skills, knowledge and behaviours that they want to test, and in addition to organizational competencies they may also be looking for **other traits,** such as:

* leadership ability
* charisma
* degree of anxiety
* integrity
* creativity
* diplomacy
* being a self-starter
* ability in personal reflection
* your 'fit' for the organization.

Bullet Guide: Tackling Tough Interview Questions

Assessment centre questions

Process questions

Some of the questions will relate to the activities (or 'process'). For example:

* *'What did you think was the most testing aspect of that last activity?'*
* *'Were you happy with your performance in the last activity?'*
* *'How do you feel about the day so far?'*
* *'Are you particularly happy or not about your performance so far?'*

The key here is to stop for a moment and think through each question for the **implications** of your response, before answering it as honestly and diplomatically as possible.

> ## 'Each excellent thing, once learned, serves for a measure of all other knowledge.'
> Philip Sidney

Written questions

Written questions may form part of an assessment centre. They are usually **related to the business** and may assume that you have done some prior homework on the company, or know that area of business well. For example:

* *'If you wanted to introduce a quality award in this organization, how would you plan its introduction?'*
* *'If you felt strongly that the company was moving in the wrong direction strategically, how would you go about influencing the key players?'*
* *'A team under your management is seriously underperforming. What would you do?'*
* *'How would you evaluate the strengths and weaknesses of a potential marketing strategy for your product?'*

Interview questions

Many interview questions have been covered already throughout this book, but **other questions** you may encounter at an assessment centre may include the following:

* 'What is it about you that pushes you to the head in this race?'
* 'What one thing do you want to tell us about yourself that you feel we may have missed out on?'
* 'What do you believe will be the most challenging part of the job for you personally?'
* 'What pushes your "hot buttons" and how do you remain in control?'
* 'How do you cope with stress?'

Top tip

Before you go to the assessment centre, find out the format of the event, who will be assessing, what qualities they are looking for and whether you have to prepare anything beforehand.

More process questions

Some of these were listed earlier in this chapter. Other examples include:

* *'What do you think of the calibre of your fellow candidates?'*
* *'Apart from yourself, to whom would you give the job, and why?'*
* *'Do you think you have been treated fairly today?'*
* *'From what you have seen, if you had to eliminate one person today, who would that be?'*
* *'What do you think we were looking for in that last exercise?'*

● *'If you had to eliminate one person, who would it be?'*

Case study

Amira has not been to an assessment centre before, but has had many interviews and thinks that this must be similar. She is shocked to find how stretched she is. She wishes she had done more research into the company – they asked her serious questions about what she would do there, not just about herself.

James does a lot of research before going to the assessment centre. He is excited and on his toes, and realizes that, even when chatting between exercises, he is being assessed. He thinks assessment centres are a good way of measuring managers from many different angles – and tells the staff this. The interviewer is impressed.

What next?

In this book I have tried to give you not only examples of tough interview **questions** but also some of the **strategies** that interviewers use when formulating their questions. I hope the examples I have given will be enough for most situations, but if not, where do you go from here?

You may find these books and websites useful:

* Hoevemeyer, Victoria A., *High-Impact Interview Questions* (New York: Amacom, 2005)
* Popovich, Igor, *Winning at Job Interviews* (London: Hodder, Teach Yourself, 2003)
* The Chartered Management Institute at http://www.managers.org.uk
* The Chartered Institute of Personnel Development at http://www.cipd.co.uk.